Moontoons Jokes & Riddles

Compiled by Robert Vitarelli

Cartoons by Marvin Townsend

American Education Publications / A Xerox Company
Middletown, Connecticut

"I should say I do remember 1969! That's the year we put a man on the moon and Dad bought us a color TV set."

Two astronauts were riding in a rocket. Unfortunately, one fell out.
Fortunately, there was a big pile of leaves below him.
Unfortunately, there was a rock in the pile of leaves.
Fortunately, he missed the rock.
Unfortunately, he missed the pile of leaves.

Question: Why did the cow jump over the moon?
Answer: Because she couldn't fly.

Astronaut: Do you wanna fly?
Junior Astronaut: Sure!
Astronaut: Wait, I'll catch one for you.

Question: Why do they call that astronaut Sunny?
Answer: Because he's so bright.

Man: Why did the Martian put a clock in his flying saucer?
Woman: Because he wanted to see time fly!

"We must be expected! One of them is holding a light for us."

"They can't be too bright! Look how cockeyed they put up their buildings."

"There! That should make them feel at home."

Question: What colors would you paint the sun and the wind?
Answer: The sun rose and the wind blue.

Question: If Earth elephants hide in trees, where do moon elephants hide?
Answer: Everyone knows there are no trees on the moon!

Boy: Why does the moon travel around the Earth every month?
Girl: Because it doesn't have much else to do!

Question: Why does Jupiter have 12 moons orbiting around it?
Answer: Because it has a lot of pull!

Little Boy: There's a planet in our house!
Mommy: That's not true.
Little Boy: Yes it is. Mercury is in our thermometer!

"Let's buzz the earth! I'm going luny stuck on this rock day in and day out!"

"Look, a hole in one!"

"You have to admire his confidence."

"Wow! Wouldn't you like to be able to stick around and see what hatches out of that egg?"

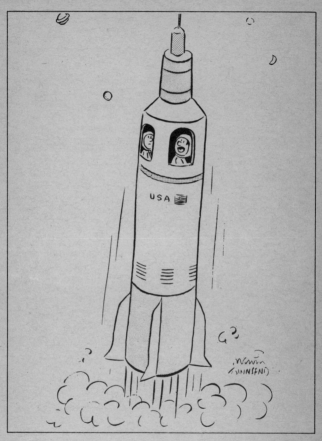

"Quick, contact control headquarters! We forgot to ask which moon—Jupiter's, Mars', Neptune's, Saturn's or the Earth's."

Boy: The teacher got mad because I didn't know where the planets were.
Mother: Next time try to remember where you put things!

Question: What kind of paper makes the best rockets?
Answer: Flypaper!

Bill: How do you make the world spin backwards?
Nell: Put it in revearth.

Question: What did one lost hunter say to the other while wandering through the dark forest?
Answer: Satellite I see ahead?

Question: What do astronauts eat after breakfast and before dinner?
Answer: Launch.

"It was a great accomplishment all right—but I happen to know they had a certain cow pioneer the way for them."

"They call themselves a 'moon-rock' group."

Question: How do rocket pilots read their flight manuals?
Answer: From hover to hover.

Question: How did the hippie rocket get to the moon?
Answer: Flower Power.

Woman to Grocer: Meat is so high. When was beef the highest?
Grocer: When the cow jumped over the moon.

Boy: How far does light travel?
Girl: I don't know. But it gets here too early in the morning.

X: How many balls of string would it take to reach the moon?
Y: One—but it has to be a very big one.

"This is my first moon flight—what is the movie?"

Astronaut: When do I get to go up in space?
Big Boss: When the chimps are down.

Psychiatrist: Are you coming or going?
Astronaut: If I knew that, I wouldn't be here!

Wife of Astronaut: My husband writes that he's all unstrung over his next flight.
Friend: Why don't you send him a wire?

Martian: There are beds all over Mars.
Earthman: That sounds like a lot of bunk to me!

Question: What did the Martian see in his frying pan?
Answer: An unidentified frying object.

Question: If newlyweds on Earth go on honeymoons, where do newlyweds go on the moon?
Answer: On honeyearths!

"Either there are bugs on our lens or the moon is inhabited with monsters!"

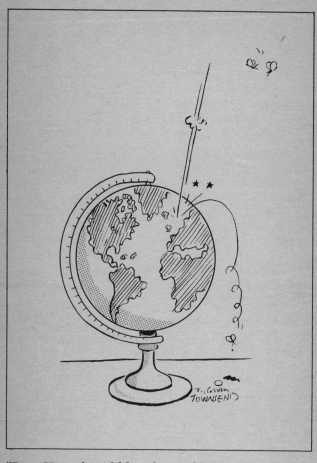

"Poor Henry! I told him he couldn't make a splash-down on it."

"We've traveled less than a quarter of a million miles, and already I miss the noises of the city, the smog, traffic jams. . ."

Question: Why is the moon landing like a chalk board?
Answer: Both are remarkable.

Question: Why is a space capsule like the Wells Fargo of the Old West?
Answer: Both need stages to carry their males (mails).

Question: What do you call the man who fires all the rockets?
Answer: Sir Launchalot.

Question: How does the sun defend itself?
Answer: With its ray gun.

Question: When do space children go to school?
Answer: Moonday through Saturnday.

Question: Who is the spaceman's favorite TV star?
Answer: Dean Martian.

"We were wondering, would you tell us what spray you use to combat the Hessian fly?"

"Take me to your feeder."

"Don't get so excited! We already knew by looking through the telescope there were a few little crawfish up here."

Man: If you saw Martians on Earth, what would you think?
Woman: I'd think we were in a lot of trouble.

Question: How would you recognize an elephant on the moon?
Answer: He'd have a big E on his spacesuit.

Boy: Who is the oldest settler in the West?
Girl: The sun.

Martian: Want to hear a couple of dillies?
Earthman: Sure!
Martian: Dilly, dilly!

Starlight, Starbright,
First star I see tonight,
I wish I may, I wish . . .
Oh, shucks, it's only a satellite!

"Frankly, the moon isn't nearly as romantic as I had always pictured it."

"This moonlighting is wearing me out!"

"Forget the moon rocks! I found some moon-eye agate marbles."

Man: How's business?
Astronomer: Looking up!

Girl: Do you know there's a dog star?
Boy: Are you Sirius?

Question: What's purple and goes broosh?
Answer: A space plum.

Boy: What did the hippie say to the invisible Martian?
Girl: You're outtasite, man!

Question: Why did Mickey Mouse go into outer space?
Answer: To find Pluto.

Question: What happens when you cross a stupid elephant with a rocket?
Answer: You get a big rocket that forgets where it's going!

"I guess it's only fair."

"I'm afraid they flew so low the heat from it popped our entire field of corn!"

Question: What is green with polka dots?
Answer: A Martian with measles.

Question: Where does a witch keep her spaceship?
Answer: In her broom closet!

Daffynition: Space station.
Answer: Rocket parkarama.

There was a young spaceman named Rollo,
Who joined up with the crew of Apollo.
Just one day in flight,
Seemed such a fright,
That Rollo jumped out of Apollo.

As the capsule fell wildly toward the sea, one of
the astronauts said, "Boy, I bet half the people
down there think we're going to crash!"
His partner said, "Yep, and so do half the people
up here!"

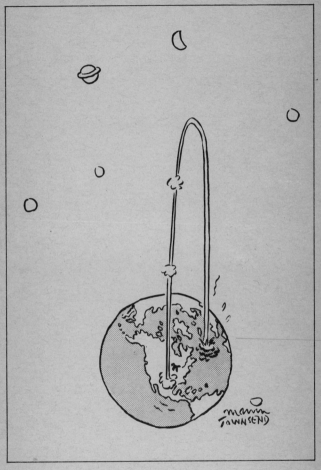

"Oh, well! You can't win 'em all."

"They haven't even landed yet and already they're causing air pollution!"

"I certainly hope you people don't treat us the way you did the American Indian."

Boy: Can you change the full moon for me, Sir?
Clerk: Now how can I change the moon for you?
Boy: Easy! Just give me four quarters!

Big Boss: Well, we've saved enough money to get you to the moon.
Astronaut: Wow! When can I go?
Big Boss: When we save enough to get you back to Earth!

Question: Why are astronauts Roman?
Answer: They go Roman all around in space.

Scientist: That astronaut is like a spinning wheel.
Man: Why?
Scientist: Because he spins some great yarns!

Astronaut: That was a close call. We had to live on one tiny cube of space food for three days.
Interested Man: Weren't you afraid you'd fall off?

"I don't suppose we'll ever find out how this got buried here."

"H'm'm! Whites whiter and colors brighter! We've just got to find out what kind of detergent they use."

"Are you sure these rubber inner tubes are strong enough to thrust me 238,856 miles?"

Question: What does an astronaut put in a sandwich?
Answer: Launchin' meat.

Man: Why can't I buy a ticket to the moon?
Agent: Because the moon is full right now!

Question: Which weighs more, the full moon or the quarter moon?
Answer: The full moon is lighter!

Son: Dad, can I study the stars?
Rich Father: Sure! And if you really like them, I'll buy Hollywood for you.

Teacher: Harry, how can you prove the Earth is round?
Harry: I don't have to prove it. I never said it was.

"Sometimes I envy the children of the past—the simplicity of Mother Goose and the cow jumping over the moon!"

"Another great scientific discovery! She didn't complete the jump after all."

"Then it's a deal! $24 worth of trinkets for the moon!"

Question: How are tiny time pills like astronauts?
Answer: They are both found in capsules!

Question: What time is it when an elephant sits in a rocket?
Answer: Time to get a new rocket.

Bill: Why is Saturn like a bell?
Nell: There's a certain ring about it.

Boy: If sailors sing "Anchors Aweigh," what do cows sing?
Girl: Milky Way.

Woman: How do you walk in space?
Astronaut: Very carefully!

"This should shake them up a bit."

"I don't know about taking you to my leader—but I might be able to get you an audience with our Vice-President or Prime Minister."

"I am now writing with my astronaut space pen, which may be purchased at your local store for only $3.98 plus tax."

Question: What is fog?
Answer: Earth mist.
Question: What is a meteor?
Answer: Missed from space.

Young Boy: Can you sing on Neptune?
Spaceman: I don't think so. But if you'll hum a bit
of it maybe I'll try to sing along.

Question: How is the moon built like your house?
Answer: It has beams.

Question: Who would you hire to prepare a ban-
quet on the moon?
Answer: A craterer.

Earthman: Are there cows on Pluto?
Plutonian: Not that I've herd of!

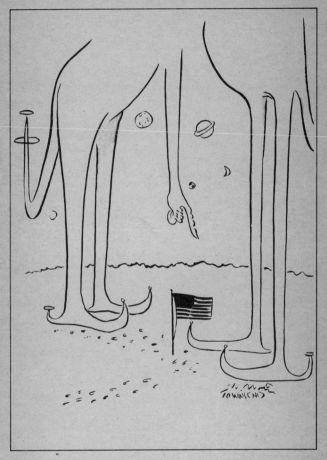

"It looks like termites, but who ever heard of termites having their own flag?"

"Oh, good! I'm glad you're out of orbit. It's time for your splash-down."

"They're certainly odd looking creatures—all head and legs."

X: He thinks like a satellite.
Y: Yes, I've heard how his mind wanders!

Boy: What was the first satellite to orbit the Earth?
Teacher: The moon.

Daffynition: Parasite.
Answer: Where parachutes land.

Teacher: Name four things in space.
Pupil: Two planets and two stars.

Question: Why do you think clouds are like people riding horses?
Answer: Because they hold the rains.

"I wonder if I could borrow 2,000 gallons of diesel fuel?"

"It's obvious they're not very far advanced in communications."

"I'm not sure, but I'd say it's some sort of an advanced space ship."

"Hang on! Here comes one."